Fuel Your Faith

A Practical Guide to Igniting a Healthy Spirituality

Jean Wise

Fuel Your Faith
A Practical Guide to Igniting a
Healthy Spirituality

Introduction

"Be sure to take the time to hike to the back meadow and walk our grass labyrinth," beckoned the retreat center guidebook.

I studied the map and set out to explore a new part of the grounds. The grassy path wound its way down towards a creek and passed through a wooded area. I listened to birds singing and the water gurgling. The sunlight danced through the trees.

I finally reached the tall grass of the meadow and began to search for the labyrinth. Instead of finding what I sought, a swarm of mosquitoes found me. Waving them away, I shivered as the light began to dim. I wondered if I could find my way back as the sun set.

About 30 minutes later, I finally returned to the retreat center, disappointed, tired, cold, and itchy. This adventure did not turn out as I expected.

Reflecting about my walk, I shook my head when I realized my hike that day mirrored my current spiritual walk. I expected a smooth journey with God, no bugs, easy path, achieving my goals, and arriving where I wanted to go.

"I don't understand, Lord. I am in such a rut. Show me the way," I lamented.

Have you ever felt this way on your faith journey? Stagnant, detached from God and hungry for more? Spiritual dry and thirsty for God? Unsatisfied, unfulfilled, and restless?

Faith is a gift from God. In God's grace, we already possess faith.

For by grace you have been saved through faith,
and this is not your own doing;
it is the gift of God
Ephesian 2: 8

We have this wonderful gift within us, but so often leave it unwrapped. How do we live with a vibrant faith? How do we fuel our faith?

Igniting a healthy spirituality is both an art and practice.

God is the creator, the center, the energy to nurture the gift of faith he planted within us. He is the art, the light, the More we seek.

Our response is the ongoing, lifelong practice of being faithful. We explore ideas and open our eyes to see his presence and our hearts to experience God in deeper ways. Spiritual practices reconnect us to the Art.

I cannot cause light.
The most I can do is put myself in the path of its beam.
Annie Dillard

Fuel Your Faith is a practical guidebook to move your soul into God's light. This book is not a deep theological discourse about spiritual disciplines, but a quick resource for ideas to stir the embers of faith God gives each of us. This book contains a potpourri of approaches to move you from stuck to unstuck and from chilliness to the warmth, power, and comfort of a blazing fire.

Not all ideas found in this book will fit everyone. Stay open, experiment. What doesn't work now may work in a different season of life for you. I encourage you to explore and experiment, but know not all ideas will resonate with you.

Remember God is the fire. We cannot begin to contain him, to harness him, or to control the heat of his spirit. But we can nurture the sparks, awaken our conscious, and open the flue of our hearts to let his light inward to our souls.

We can cultivate a healthy spirituality. God wants our faith to grow and our lives to glow with his love. What a marvelous gift God gives us – let's enter the Light and fan the flames of our faith.

Chapter 1 – The Flame of Prayer

If you are too busy to pray,
You are too busy.
Anonymous

How do you start a fire? Most survival guides tell us the first step is to gather tinder and kindling. Tinder is the dry twigs and small leaves used to strengthen the initial spark of a fire. Next kindling, the larger sticks, are added for the blaze to grow and flourish.

Start slow. Intentionally, we fuel the fire with ordinary, mundane items found in our faith forest. Prayer is the essential tinder and kindling for igniting a healthy spirituality.

Most believers want to experience God deeply in prayer. I hear this desire to be closer to God with my spiritual direction clients, in small groups, among those on retreat, and in my blog readers' comments.

As I reread my journals and uncover my own deepest desire, the continual contact with our Creator is a hunger I feel within my soul. One of my ongoing prayers comes from Psalm 86:11:

Teach me your way, Lord,
that I may rely on your faithfulness;
give me an undivided heart,
that I may fear your name.

We want to know God as he wants to know us. He is a loving Creator who wants to be with us. A God who desires a deep relationship with us as much as we yearn for him.

What you seek,
is seeking you.
Rumi

Sharing a deep desire to stay consistent and focused on God during the daily grind, distractions, and detours we face, we hunger to draw closer to him, not be sidetracked.

We yearn to remember and stay mindful of God. We want this closeness when we don't feel loved and valued by others. The craving to be more aware of his presence and to know God is with us in health challenges and family difficulties highlights the chill in our soul.

Prayer is the spark that starts our soul ablaze. The warm glow of prayer lights our path to God.

Prayer ignites the fire of faith.

What is Prayer

Prayer is talking and listening to God. It is a sacred conversation among two beings who love each other.

Consider how amazing this gift of prayer is: The Lord himself wants to be with us, hear from us, guide us, and love us.

Too often my prayers consist of requests, pleas, even demands. Like a spoiled toddler who thinks the world evolves around her, I focus on my needs. I am slowly reminding myself God is not just a vending machine.

Prayer realigns my focus on God alone.

Prayer deepens when we understand why we pray and its importance becomes clearer.

Here are five reasons to explore prayer. These motivations form the acronym: DEPTH:

1. D - Discover. Prayer helps me hear my voice, name my deeper desire, and discover God's presence within me. As I find the words to express to God what I am experiencing, I gain self-insight and often uncover God's guidance and direction.

2. E - Experience. Prayer slows me down. I run ahead of my thoughts and outrun my words. I overthink and get ahead of myself, rushing with worry and fear and trying to do everything and control everything all by myself. Prayer helps me savor God, worship him, and linger in his presence. Prayer builds my relationship with him, like kindling stirs a fire.

3. P - Persevere. I gain hope and strength in my time with God. Thank heaven we have a forgiving divine Being who understands our distractions and our failed intentions to be with him. If I skip my morning prayers for several weeks, forget to thank him each day, and neglect coming to him first with my ideas and commitments, God welcomes me back into his presence. Each time I enter his love and allow myself to be held, formed, and awakened, my devotion to remain with him increases.

4. T - Transformed by love. Experiencing God's love helps me love others. I am slowly learning to care for and see them through the eyes and heart of God. Prayer increases compassion for both myself and those I serve. Being with God in prayer brings forgiveness for my sins which in turn helps me forgive others. When I reread my journaled prayers, I often come back to the same issues repeatedly, but each time in a different way. God slowly transforms us into his masterpieces.

5. H - Hear God. The way I best hear God, his wisdom, his love, and his guidance is through prayer. His words of affirmation, gentle corrections, and light for my next steps leads my

way. Through prayer I become quiet and still to hear his whisper.

The purpose of prayer is to share ourselves with the God extraordinaire.

There are many books on prayer but in this book, I would like to give you practical tips for igniting your prayer life. Like the tinder and kindling, steps for prayer involves simple systems and sparks.

Start with the Basics

Assess what you are doing now in prayer. What is working? What isn't working? Be honest. Talk with God about your desire to deepen your conversation with him.

We can read all the books about prayer. We attend worship and seminars about talking with God. We fill our heads with the what's and the to do's, but we fail to simply pray.

Just start where you are now and pray. Don't rush. Linger with God. Pray.

Learn and experiment with new ways of praying that inspire our connection with God. Here are examples of various styles of prayers:
- breath prayers
- centering prayers
- welcoming prayers
- prayer of relinquishment
- healing prayers
- praying the scriptures
- prayer of examen,
- walking a labyrinth.

Find a chapter or verse from the Bible and rewrite it your own words. The book of Psalms works extremely well for this idea. For example, the opening line of the 23rd Psalm forms this prayer: "The Lord is my shepherd, my guide, my helper. I never need or desire anything else except for God." The Bible is the living word of God and we are invited to explore its contents for nourishment for our journey.

What do you experience with your senses? Notice your surroundings. Pay attention.

A change in location often refreshes the spirit. Go on a retreat. Walk your neighborhood. Enjoy the woods, a park, or even your own backyard. Look up. Listen. Take a deep breath.

Experience God in nature. I like to sit on my backyard deck in summer. In winter, I enjoy watching the birds in the feeder outside my office window. I often plan an afternoon walk in the nearby woods or visit an arboretum.

Freshen Up your Prayer Space or Try a New Time of Day

Create a home altar and a sacred space at home for your prayer time. Light a candle. Try soft background music. Decorate an altar with a cross, painting, and symbolic meaningful items. Change the colors of the cloth in your space to match the church calendar colors, such as blue for Advent or purple for Lent.

Adjust the times you pray or try praying the liturgical hours - morning, noon, afternoon, and evening. Notice how the shadows and light affect your prayers. How do you feel when you pause to be with God?

Creating space for God not only physically, but in your schedule and your heart draws us nearer to him.

Inner space is a place of peace. My heart becomes a portable sanctuary where I experience God even in the crazy chaos and cares of living.

This center within me is a safe dwelling where I can say anything to God, knowing he understands and hears me. I long to be in this inner sacred place where I feel loved and accepted by God.

I am going to be honest. I struggle with living and resting within this inner sacred space, but I am learning to linger there longer and come back to it more often. Life's journey travels along a spiral path, ever drawing us closer to God. I am gentle with myself as I step in closer to my heart and the heart of God.

Here are a few tips for venturing into an inner sacred space with God:

- Rituals invite me into silence and stillness. I bow and ask God to be present with me. I take a few deep breaths. Other ideas are: beginning with a favorite breath prayer, lighting a candle, and/or playing soft music.
- Read the scriptures. Linger with one verse. I find writing my prayers and current experiences in a journal deepens my time with God.
- Routines of good sleep, staying nourished, well-hydrated, and walking. Good self-care of my body complements good soul-care.
- Reduce time in cyberspace. The chatter of social media and endless rabbit trails of the Internet distract me. Turning down the volume of my email chirps and placing boundaries on my computer usage creates more time to be with God.
- Reading settles my spirit into hearing God. Spending time with my Bible, an inspirational devotional, and spiritual writings from other sojourners, both living and dead, gives me new perspectives, helps me articulate what I am experiencing, and offers new ideas to explore.
- Recognize what is going on within our hearts. Pay attention and name the feelings. Hear your own voice without the influence of others and the noise from outside. Just talk with Jesus. Don't make it

too complicated with churchy words and what you think you are supposed to say. A few years ago, I experienced this type of inner work on a retreat with the help of God and a spiritual director. Slowly I unwrapped my fears and hurts to identify the core emotion of feeling abandoned and how that ruled my behavior. I presented my sense of abandonment to God, who healed my brokenness with his love. Inner work can be difficult, but will yield more space for God in our hearts.

- Reflect about your heart. Imagine your heart. See it uncluttered and God present. How does Christ sit with you?

Sparks to Start and Sustain

What reminds you to pray? A trigger directs our heart and mind to God. What triggers occur in your life helping you remember God?

The sight of empty bird nests perched on the barren trees in winter remind me to pray.

Winter used to be my least favorite season. That time of year enfolded me with a sense of emptiness and hopelessness. My mood reflected the dreary gray winter sky that blanketed northwest Ohio.

But the last few years I see winter with new eyes and a renewed appreciation of its beauty and purpose. I am surprised at this phenomenon and the joy I discovered in its stark loveliness.

Bird nests became the first indication of seeing winter in a fresh way and became a trigger for conversations with God.

My eyes were drawn to them. I saw them everywhere. Tree branches, now barren, allowed me to see them where they were once hidden.

Every time I looked up, multiple bird nests materialized. They beckoned me, "Look at me, I have something to tell you." In his mysterious way, God began to invite me to wonder about these empty and barren nests. God and I talked about the message in the bird nests in my times of prayer with him.

I listened to his lessons:

The nests were not just barren, but represented hollow vacant cups, waiting to be filled. Instead of focusing on what they did not have, they remained open, ready to hold new life that was yet to come. These ordinary nests made of everyday stuff, though empty, slowly pulled me into a transformational lesson for me.

The nests embodied God's promise of fresh beginnings in the next season. That simple change in my perspective permeated my soul. My feelings of being mired in dreariness and dryness disappeared. For the first time in a long time, I felt hope.

The bird nests served as a trigger to enter God's presence, even in the dreary season of winter. The nests reminded me to pray. They appeared as prayer prompts during the day.

Prayer prompts are the common recurring objects, places, and times during our day providing cues to pray. Train yourself to watch for them and over time these simple moments draw your attention to God moments.

Here are a few prayer prompts that may help remind you to pray:

- Stopping at traffic light.
- Hearing a certain song on your play list.

- Noticing the blare of an emergency siren.
- Going up or down stairs.
- Turning the sound off during a TV commercial.
- Reaching for a towel.
- Reading the newspapers, the news online, or listening to the news.
- Driving past a church or a friend's house.
- Brushing your teeth.

God sends his Holy Spirit to fuel our faith in mighty ways. Ask him to teach you how to pray. Tell him you want to grow closer to him and hear his voice. Make the commitment to spend time in prayer and watch for prayer moments throughout the day.

> *My sheep listen to my voice; I know them,*
> *and they follow me.*
> *John 10: 27*

The foundation of a life-giving fire begins with the act of slowly building the blaze with tinder and kindling. The foundation of our faith starts with prayer in spending time with God, being open to his lessons, and willing to grow as he leads. Prayer will ignite and fuel your faith for eternity.

> *It is only when the whole heart is gripped with the*
> *passion of prayer that the life-giving fire descends, for*
> *none but the earnest man gets access to the ear of God.*
> *E.M. Bounds*

Fan the Flames of Prayer Refection Questions:

1. What helps you to pray?
2. What prayer triggers remind you to pray?
3. What will be your next step in spending more time in prayer?

Prayer

Lord God of all fire, thank you for wanting to be with us through prayer. We ask that our desire to listen to you draws us nearer to you and opens our heart to hear your voice. Thank you for always welcoming us in prayer.

Chapter 2 – The Flame of Study

Read with a vulnerable heart. Expect to be blessed in the readings.
Read as one awake, one waiting for the beloved. Read with reverence.
Macrina Wiederkehr

My spiritual director asked me how I visualized my faith. The surprising answer tumbled out of my mouth as I told her I pictured an hour glass.

"What does that image mean to you?" she asked.

I thought a few minutes searching for the words to express why this image emerged. Then I explained to both to her and to myself as if I was hearing it for the first time.

"Often I feel I know God in my head and sometimes I experience him in my heart. But most of the time my faith is disjointed – separated like a tiny constriction between the two, like an hourglass."

She nodded and said with a smile. "You need a new image. What would you want your faith to be look like?"

It didn't take me long to answer: A tree.

I love the vision of a tree. This miracle of nature has an assortment of roots reaching deep into the ground. The solid foundation of the tree anchored with long tubers and numerous off growths extending in different directions offers strength and hope. New young offshoots, green with new life and eagerness to grow, also add nourishment to its life.

The branches reach upward, praising their creator, and bearing fruit. The leaves bask and drink in the sunshine. Tiny cells within the plant labor to produce energy and food for growth. Tree limbs also provide shade, beauty, and homes for other creatures.

Both branches and roots sustain each other. The roots provide nourishment. The branches provide light and the leaves supply the chlorophyll. A sturdy trunk connects to the two, supporting an open current of sustenance back and forth between the head and the heart.

A tree represents a healthy faith. Fuel for the growth of all living things and fuel for our faith is the spiritual practice of study. Study nurtures both the mind and the heart and fosters our faith forward.

As prayer is the bones of our faith, scripture and study serve as the muscles.

What is Study

Study is the selection and reflection of what we find to connect and direct our heart and mind.

Like eating junk food, we can nourish our minds and heart with shallow, mindless garbage. Study is the intentional focus of what will stretch us, cultivate us, and form us more like God. Good material provides meat to make us think with our brains and strength to our muscles.

Study stirs our imagination and opens us to wonder. With study, we gain new ways to see God's world and gain skills to enter new possibilities. Study is the nourishment to enlarge our hearts with compassion and service.

Healthy Nourishment, not Junk Food

To fully feed our heart and mind, we need to input healthy nutrients. Everyone enjoys an occasional treat of junk food or mindless activity, but a steady stream of garbage leads to a dump.

Developing the practice of study involves digging into the scriptures and reading inspiring books. We think about and plow into the meaning of the word. We allow our brains to ponder new perspectives, to stretch and grow, and even change.

We make connections between past experiences, what we see currently and then wonder what the study could mean for us in the future. We choose what we will do with the information. Will we offer it to someone or continue to sit with the information for our own use?

Study is the process of taking in, wondering and pondering, digesting, and applying to our life.

Study could mean choosing a theme for the year. Then we could find good resources to underline and explore the theme with others. Maybe take a class. Keep recording notes and journal the lessons or nuggets of truth you are gleaning from this material. Create your own study notes as if you were sitting in a class with God as the teacher.

I started a bullet journal last year, a simple lined notebook. Within its pages, I list the books I read. When I finish a book, I write down the title, author, date I read it, and key points and quotes I want to remember. Next, I write a small summary of my yearly reading, and what wisdom I discovered that year. This recording helps me digest and remember the words I read.

Going deeper leads us to the questions: Are we studying for information or transformation? How do we open our hearts and mind to God's school of transformation?

We fail in our duty to study God's Word not so much because it is difficult to understand, not so much because it is dull and boring, but because it is work. Our problem is not a lack of intelligence or a lack of passion. Our problem is that we are lazy.
R.C. Sproul

The Value of Asking Questions

Questions grow from curiosity. Why do we as adults neglect to use the gift of wonder? We lose the childlike marvel as we age. Remember how young kids and students ask questions all the time? Questions are a powerful spiritual tool to hear God and to stretch and grow the flame of our faith.

For a long time, I thought life consisted of finding the answers and playing by those rules. I didn't like the tension between the certainty of knowing and the living in the gray area of unknowing. I used to seek the supremacy of feeling I am in control and the appearance of having my act together, wearing the prettiest mask for others to see.

Questions leave us unsettled and searching. They remind us we are not in control. Questions magnify the truth that we already know we don't know. Sometimes we like the comfort of what we know and the black and white of predictability. Questions rouse us from our comfort zones to enter the unfamiliar mystery of life and faith.

As I gain the wisdom of the second half of life (at least I hope I am learning), I find I like to stay with the questions longer. I linger in their unfolding. I hold the green bud of curiosity. Questions help me to take that second bite of an emotion or situation and allow it to slowly melt in my consciousness. Growth tastes better after simmering than a quick microwavable tasteless answer.

It seems to me Lord that we search much too desperately for answers, when a good question holds as much grace as an answer. Jesus, you are the Great Questioner. Keep our questions alive, that we may always be seekers rather than settlers. Guard us well from the sin of settling in with our answers hugged to our breasts. Make of us a wondering, far-sighted, questioning, restless people And give us the feet of pilgrims on this journey unfinished.

Macrina Wiederkehr

Questions fuel our curiosity leading to new ideas and insights. Insurmountable problems now hold possible solutions. Answers lure us into comfort ruts while questions energize us to explore deeper and to enter newer horizons.

Instead of rushing to answers, lingering longer with questions empowers and enables us to keep moving forward into new territory. We discover we have more courage than we thought. We deepen our roots of faith. We dwell in hope. We find God present, even in the unknown. We thrive in the powerful possibilities of pondering questions.

Confidence, like art, never comes from having all the answers;
it comes from being open to all the questions.
Earl Gray Stevens

Here are examples of questions to use in the practice of study:

- **Where am I right now?** I like how God in the book of Genesis looks for Adam and Eve, already knowing where they are and what they have done. Yet he asked, "Where are you?" I ask this question most days in my morning time with God and just the question, not necessarily the answer, guides my prayer.

- **What is the invitation in this emotion/circumstance/word/interaction?** What is God unfolding for me to receive? Am I willing and ready to receive his gift? I am not good at naming my emotions. I like to stuff them under food and busyness instead of holding them in my hand and learning from them. When I ask these questions, I deal better with what is stirring in my heart.
- **Am I asking the right question?** Not "why does this always happen to me?" but reframing my negative self-talk into truth, not lies.
- **What am I learning?** How am I stimulating my brain and discovering new thoughts? Last year I took an online course from Denmark about Hans Christian Andersen and how we as writers, craft folktales. The class was fun, stimulating, and ignited my brain's synapses for new connections and creativity.
- **What are my options**? Multiple options exist if we only seek them.
- **What am I most grateful for? What am I the least grateful for?**
- **What has worked for me before and how can I bring more lessons from my past successes into my life now? What is no longer working and needs to be released?**
- **What if?**
- **What is the worse that could happen? What if I fail? What if I succeed?**
- **What does this make possible?**
- **What draws me away from God or towards God?**
- **What will nourish my soul?**
- **How do I best show love in this situation? Be love?**
- **How can I better understand?**
- **What question is bubbling up within me or around me right now?**

Be patient toward all that is unsolved in your heart and try to love the questions themselves, like locked rooms and like books that are now written in a very foreign tongue.

Do not now seek the answers, which cannot be given you because you would not be able to live them.

And the point is, to live everything.

Live the questions now.

Perhaps you will then gradually, without noticing it, live along some distant day into the answer.

Rilke

Using Lectio Divina in Study

Lectio divina is an approach to study as a spiritual practice. Lectio Divina means "spiritual reading" and follows a classical pattern of slow reading, rereading, meditating, and contemplating the material. Study deepens with repetition, articulation in our own words, and identification of the lessons learned. We allow the word to take us out of our own agenda and open our heart to what God is saying to us.

Marjorie Thompson described lectio divina as a dance, *"the sacred movement of the divine-human relationship."* This dance, this back and forth movement between us and the Holy, refreshes our spirit and leads us into deeper knowledge with God.

We weave back and forth with a reading or new learning, shifting, and turning meaning into the words or experience, then allowing our whole being, the head and heart, to embrace the dance. Lectio divina fuels our faith by opening our hearts to God's wisdom for us.

I use the lectio divina rhythm to study the scripture but am also learning to apply this technique to other area such as inspirational books, movies, nature, and even life events.

Nobody ever outgrows Scripture; the book widens and deepens with our years.
Charles Spurgeon

The four steps of lectio divina are simple and easy to follow. Begin by choosing a scripture passage, then read the verse(s) four times, pausing in silence between each time.

1. Read the word of God slowly and reverently. Allow the words to sink into your heart. Note any words resonating with you. Sometime a phrase may even stir a resistance or agitation within your spirit.
2. The second step is reflection or meditation about the word of God. Think about the text. Consider its meaning. Wonder why that word or phrase echoed in your soul.
3. Next is our response to what we are learning. Don't overthink, just talk with God about this passage and what it says to you. Find the words to describe what you are feeling.
4. The last step is to rest or contemplate, letting go of our expectations and being still before God. His whispered wisdom in this learning nurtures our transformation.

The most foolish person in the world is the one who has the opportunity to read, absorb, digest, live in, be immersed in worship-reading the Bible, but doesn't do it because of preoccupation with other things of this world.
Rex B. Andrews

Lectio Divina can be used individually or in a small group and is a powerful and intimate study tool to fuel our faith. Use these steps as guidelines, ever being open to where God leads you.

Be curious. Keep open to learning. God gives us a world to explore with unknowns yet to discover and to use. Grow your mind and heart with study. Fuel your faith.

The word of scripture should never stop sounding in our ears and working in you all day long, just like the words of someone you love. Do not ask 'how shall I pass this on? But "what does it say to me? Then ponder this word long in your heart until it has gone right into you and taken possession of you.
Dietrich Bonhoeffer

Fan the Flame of Study Reflection Questions

1. What will you learn in the next 30 days? What topic could be adopted for a yearlong study?
2. What books do you want to read that will bring good nourishment both to your mind and your heart?
3. How will you apply Lectio Divina to your study?

Prayer

Lord of Wisdom, nourish our minds and our hearts with your word. Open us to receive new knowledge transforming us into who you want us to become.

Chapter 3 - The Flame of Celebration

Joy is the serious business of heaven.
C. S. Lewis.

I can't remember exactly how old I was, four or five. I sauntered ahead of my mom on the sidewalk as she chatted with her friend and walking companion. I wasn't paying much attention to what they were saying until I heard my name mentioned.

"I worry about your daughter," said the friend. "She is such a somber child. Never smiles."

What me? Those words seared my heart and became part of my story.

A few years ago, I participated in a life assessment where you evaluate various aspects of your life using a scale of one to ten. The score of ten was given to the parts where you felt you lived life to the fullest.

You know these kinds of tests. They look something like this: Rate yourself in the following categories from one, being the lowest/weakest to 10, being the highest. Life areas assessed are categories such as physical, mental, emotional, social, financial, spiritual, family, joy/recreation, personal growth, time, career, etc. They may be listed in a bulleted checklist or a wheel.

I enjoy taking these *"peeks inside of my life"* quizzes. It affirms what I know about myself and often gives me a new perspective about why I do or think certain ways.

The results of the most recent test rested before me. I could guess the score already, as this was the third time I completed one of these self-identity tools.

My lowest? My "F" in the report card of life? My "why can't you do better" score? My weakest qualities fall under the category of joy and recreation.

I flunk celebration. My assessment shows I am lopsided in the joy department. I race from one completed job to another without stopping to enjoy the accomplishment. When I retired from public health, they practically had to drag me to my own party. On the last day of my work, I slipped out the back door early to avoid the good-byes.

I continued to live the story started when I was young – somber, no joy. I used the excuse of *"God just wired me this way with intense focus"* and offered no patience with frivolous celebration.

Yet every time I completed one of those assessments, I heard God's gentle invitation to grow in this discipline. My soul hungers for the joy, the delight, the dance with God in celebration. A piece was missing from my life. My flame of faith darkened without the addition of the colors of celebration.

I decided to select the word *joy* as my word of the year one January and to intentionally discover delight.

I explored the idea of joy. I embraced the present when I was with others. I paused and smiled at my grandkids' laughter. I gazed at the face of my newborn grandson. I relished moments of peace and companionship. I practiced joy and celebrated life.

Celebration fueled my faith and drew me closer to God. I intentionally chose joy. Now I deliberately find moments to celebrate life, transitions, and ordinary glimpses of heaven.

The Joy of Celebration

Jesus began his life with joy.

But the angel said to them, "Do not be afraid. I bring
you good news that will cause great joy
for all the people."
Luke 2: 10

Jesus left his human journey with an eternal legacy in the gift of joy.

I have told you this so that my joy may be in you and
that your joy may be complete.
John 15: 11

The Bible overflows with celebration.
- Marian and her friends danced with their tambourines after escaping from Egypt.
- The angels sang when Jesus was born.
- Jesus turned the water into wine so the party could continue.

When we celebrate, we turn our hearts towards the God who gives us all things. Our spirit lifts and we gain strength and energy to continue our life journey.

Celebration brings joy to others and enhances our worship. Celebration connects us with friends and family when we share together in jubilation. The book of Nehemiah reminds us that *"the joy of the Lord is our strength."*

When Paul listed the fruit of the Holy Spirit, joy is number two following love. I wonder if that highlights the important status of joy and celebration in our walk through life.

But the fruit of the Spirit is love, joy,
peace, forbearance, kindness, goodness,
faithfulness, gentleness, and self-control. Against such
things there is no law.
Gal. 5: 22-23

The practice of celebration brings energy, strength, and endurance. We enjoy the presence of the Lord within our hearts. We learn to relax and laugh at ourselves. Joy adds color and vitality to our faith.

Joy, not grit, is the hallmark of holy obedience. We need to be light-hearted in what we do to avoid taking ourselves too seriously.
It is a cheerful revolt against self and pride.
Richard J. Foster

How to Build Joy in our Lives

Building joy and celebration in our lives begins with the intention of finding, fostering, and sharing joy. We decide joy is an important ingredient in our faith and actively seek ways to increase this emotion in our hearts.

Joy is an essential trait in a healthy spirituality and will fuel our faith as well as the faith of others. Too many Christians are gloomy and solemn. They lose the childlike faith of fully plunging into God's arms and trusting him without regrets.

Joy is prayer; joy is strength: joy is love; joy is a net of love by which you can catch souls.
Mother Teresa

Ever add "fire enhancers" to a bonfire? These chemicals cause the flames to dance with shades of blues, reds, purples, and greens. Suddenly we see color where we didn't before. Focusing on celebration and deliberately seeking ways to practice this discipline in our lives, our souls come alive with the colors of joy.

Here are six ways to cultivate joy in your life, using the acronym of PRAISE:

P – Pray first. Always begin with prayer, asking God for the gift of joy. Come to God requesting an increased awareness of opportunities for celebration. Seek new eyes to discover joy all around you wherever you are.

R – Reframe with musical refrains. Music adds joy and enhances the delight in our faith walk. I like to use lyrics of songs as prayers. Listening to music rocks and soothes our souls like babies in the arms of their mother.

> Music expresses joy for us. Invites us to come along with its beat, dancing to celebrate good times and twirling away our troubles. The beat of a tune can raise our moods, give us energy, and lightens our step.

> Uplifting music helps us to be healthier. One study showed that after research participants listened to joyful music, their blood vessels widened by as much as 26%, a similar response seen after aerobic exercise.

> Sometimes just humming a tune brings back a good memory and a smile. Create a play list. Find a radio station with uplifting music.

> Plan fun with music. We occasionally will sing "This Little Light of Mine" in church and invite the adults to raise their index finger like a candle and bounce to the beat of the music. For our stoic traditional church, this lively music is quite the accomplishment.

A – Assess your life for the amount of celebration you experience. Like the life assessment tool, I mentioned at the beginning of this chapter, we may be surprised at how little we enjoy life. Take inventory of the joy in your life.

I – Imagine. What is your image of God? Is he a sour old man sitting far away in the corner like stern judge? That picture existed in my mind and heart starting from childhood into mid-adult life. I now keep on my desk the sketch of "Jesus Laughing." I see God much differently now.

I love finding images of Christ with a smiling and friendly face. After intentionally gazing at these friendly portraits of Jesus, my internal view of him unfolds with more joy.

S -Smile more. Are we smiling because we are happy or are we happy because we smile? The powerful act of smiling is a practice bringing delight to our spirit and to others and can transform the world.

> Just think: Smiling costs nothing. A smile takes only a quick second, but offers encouragement beyond our imagination. Smiling creates good will and joy, and nourishes relationships.

> Smiling releases endorphins throughout our bodies, making us feel relaxed and opened to joy. We look better too!

> And yes "we can fake it till we make it." Even forced smiling guides the mind to more positive thinking and lifts our moods. Once we begin to feel better, we begin to experience God's joy in new ways.

E – Evaluate what you know about celebration. Read Bible verses about joy and keep track in your joy journal where you discover joy. Savor those moments, such as the giggle of little kids or the sharing of memories with an aging loved one.

We can taste celebration in simple ways:

- Celebrate waking up each day. It's a new day. You are alive.
- Watch the sun rise or set.
- Take the time to go to a festival – try a new food, learn about a new culture or creative activity.

- Give a gift to someone for no special reason.
- Reflect on your daily blessings.

Spending time with God pondering celebration gives you nourishment for your spirit and food for thought, and will draw you closer to him. Celebration swells the flame of our faith and adds colorful delights to our hearts.

How will you practice celebration?

If you have no joy,
there's a leak in your Christianity somewhere.
Billy Sunday

Fan the Flame of Celebration Reflection Questions

1. Where is your joy leaking from your spiritual life?
2. What is your definition of joy?
3. How could celebration fuel your faith?

Prayer:

Lord of laughter and joy, we celebrate being with you and breathing in the air of life. We smile at you and feel you smiling back. Thank you for the gift of joy that sparkles our spirit and sets fire to our faith.

Chapter 4 – The Flame of Listening through Spiritual Practice of Writing

Journal writing is a voyage to the interior.
Christina Baldwin

My great Aunt Anna's small brown suitcase smells musty. With one rusty lock no longer latching completely shut and the brown pattern on the outside faded and torn, the case appears worthless. But the contents are priceless to me.

Aunt Anna's luggage holds more than 60 years of her journals. I can trace her life from 1920 in New York City as she began her studies at Columbia University, to her missionary days in China and Japan, to her later years in Florida. I hear her story through her writing about the ups and downs of living, through wars and depressions, and through losses and celebrations.

Her writing is a legacy to me and inspires me to write about my own walk with God, to listen to myself and articulate meaning in my life, and to gain understanding of my faith by the spiritual practice of writing.

Listening through the written word keeps the fire of my faith burning longer and brighter.

What is a Spiritual Journal?

A spiritual journal is a notebook or some type of recording of your faith journey. The focus is on your relationship with God, how you see life through your spirituality, and where you prayerfully think God may be inviting you in life.

A spiritual journal is not a diary, where all the nuances of daily life are documented. Significant life events or what is impacting you in ordinary living can be the framework, but the essence of what you write is through the lens of your faith. How is that event transforming you? What does God want you to learn from this situation?

Joan Chittister calls journals *"the x-rays of our souls. They refuse to let us hide from ourselves."*

Why Keep a Spiritual Journal?

Keeping a spiritual journal is prayer in writing. I collect a variety of words, quotes, insights on those pages, but most my writing expresses my conversations with God.

I see entries in my journal as markers or signposts on my path. Where was I at this time and season of life? Writing regularly helps capture my emotions, thoughts, and prayers that often slip away from my conscious, but linger in my subconscious.

A journal opens my eyes to see and ears to hear God in a tangible way.

My journal is my inner thoughts, reflections on life and my faith walk, and a companion on this earthly journey. Keeping a journal for me is an essential practice in my spirituality.

There is something about journal writing that causes us to meditate, to recommit, and to receive spiritual impressions in the process of such pondering. Frequently, you will have cause to rejoice at how the Lord has been sensitively involved in guiding and watching over you and those you love and care about.
L. Edward Brown

Here are some other reasons for keeping a journal:

- Writing helps us to articulate our relationship with God.
- Journaling gives us a place and process to organize our thoughts. Themes and patterns emerge as I write.

- Keeping a journal is a safe place to explore our hopes, dreams, fears, joys, and concerns.
- Writing provides a record for our insights and great quotes that resonate in our heart.
- A journal stores the prayers and conversations with God we have so they're not forgotten.
- This type of writing creates a time and space on a regular basis to be with God. Writing helps us make sense of life. We get so busy living life that we don't take time to step back to savor the journey.
- I hear my own voice in my journal. Too many times we are drowned out by the noise of the world and our own internal chattering. We miss our true desires and what God is whispering to us.
- Journaling helps us discover ourselves and know God better. My story within God's story. Our story within God's story.

I begin these pages for myself, in order to think out my own particular pattern of living, my individual balance of life, work, and human relationships. And since I think best with a pencil in my hand, I started to write.
Anne Morrow Lindberg

One fear keeps many people from listening through journal writing: What if someone reads my journal?

I fully expect my children to someday read my words and thus, I write accordingly. I think of my journals as a written legacy for them.

Most of the time I am 99% honest in what I record. Only occasionally have I left something out or wrote in vague terms. Just write as candid as you feel comfortable. Let vision frame your journaling, but don't let fear stop you.

Writing as spiritual practice has nothing to do with readers per se.
You aren't writing to be read;
you are writing to be freed.

Writing as spiritual practice is conspiratorial rather than inspirational.
It conspires to strip away everything you use to maintain the illusion of certainty, security and self-identity.
Where spiritual writing seeks to bind you all the more tightly to the self you imagine yourself to be, writing as spiritual practice intends to free you from it.
Rami Shapiro

14 Tips on Keeping a Spiritual Journal

1. The number one rule of keeping a spiritual journal is to date your entry. Time flies by so quickly and writing down the date of your entry serves as a guidepost on your life journey. Often, I am amazed when I reread my journal how long ago I recorded an insight. Then I feel humbled that I am still carrying the same burden I thought I let go of years before.

2. Forget grammar, spelling, and perfect handwriting. Relax and just write. Keep it simple. Keep it open and honest. This is a safe place to express yourself without worrying about getting a grade for perfection.

3. Write out your experience. Where you are hearing God or not finding him? What surprised you lately? What are your hopes, dreams, deep desires? What is drawing you closer to God? What is taking your eyes away from him?

4. What verses, words, quotes, books, friendships, trips, interactions, music are feeding your soul right now? A journal is a wonderful place to capture those nuggets of wisdom that are helping you grow spiritually. Take these spiritual insights a step further. Why at this time and place did those words impact you? What are these words telling you about yourself? About God?

5. Express your emotions. I used to tell myself not to trust my feelings and I rarely identified and befriended them. Through journaling I name what

I am experiencing. I even keep a list of different emotions folded in my journal. Sometimes finding just the right word for how I am feeling gives me the strength, the lesson, the avenue to admit the depth of that reaction. For example, instead of writing I am afraid, I may choose disrupted, immobile, vulnerable. For angry, I may write impatient or envious. Being alive can also be described as courageous, energetic, and even spunky.

6. Don't forget to write down your joys and where you are feeling gratitude. I know I am amazed when I pay attention to these surprises during an ordinary day just how much God gives us that we often don't see.

7. Journaling is prayer. I find writing out my conversations with God helps me articulate my relationship with him. Recording what I think he is saying to me brings me peace, guidance, and clarity. I write out the prayers from other people that resonated with me. I find the words to form my own intimate and honest prayers from someplace deep within me.

8. Writing in a journal helps me problem solve and discern my next step. The act of writing out a situation, finding the right words, expressing sometimes surprising emotions, exploring options and the "what if I tried this" ideas, helps me sift and sort the next direction in my life.

9. A spiritual journal isn't a day-to-day diary full of mundane details of where and what you ate and if it rained that day. On the other hand, occasionally capturing what is occurring in your life and how it affects your walk with God is a helpful practice. Write out the depth of gratitude for friendship after a wonderful meal with friends. How the smile of a grandchild warmed our heart and made us wonder how often God smiles as he watches us play at life. How the flowers in the backyard garden remind us of beauty and creativity that surrounds us.

10. A journal can be a place to express pain, sorrow, and challenges. Writing out a painful past experience sometimes helps us let go and move on. As I write, a new lesson emerges and I learn something new about myself. God continues to form me through all things and seeing my life in print reminds me of his constant presence and protection on my spiritual journey.

11. Even in times of being overwhelmed and confused, writing in short bursts helps me dump all the anxious chaos rattling in my brain and confine them on paper. Sometimes I just use lists and bullet points to clear my mind. I have learned that when I read those lists later that most of my worries and distractions were insignificant and meaningless.

12. Don't get shackled by the thought you must write daily or even weekly. I do try for every couple of weeks, but there have been times when several months went by without any writing. Instead of something more to do, think about writing in a spiritual journal as a rhythm in life. A journal is a companion to be with you, to listen, to help you find your way, and a conduit to hear God.

13. Speaking of companion, I do take my journal along with me on retreats, to presentations, and on vacations. I love capturing my reactions and experiences outside my normal routines where often the different point of view reveals new lessons.

14. Keeping a spiritual journal may be best in certain seasons of your life. I began one during my first pregnancy. I only wrote three or four entries, but those words describing that point of my life with all its hopes, dreams, and fears are priceless for me now to read. I know others journal while caring for a ill or dying loved one. Some people go through such intense times that writing out the details takes too much energy or pain, so waiting until later may be the best approach. Other people,

like my great aunt Anna, write almost daily for many years.

The two biggest "rules" about keeping a spiritual journal boil down to this:

1. Date your writing.
2. Don't make any other rules.

Deep Listening

The process of writing deepens our listening skills.

Spiritual writing expands the interior conversation of consciousness to include your relationship with the sacred. You are no longer alone on the quest, or on paper. You are in conversation with something you perceive as beyond, or deep within, yourself. It is this inclusion of the sacred that spiritualizes the writing.
Christina Baldwin

Writing reveals patterns that otherwise may be missed. Finding the words to describe an experience, slowly describing it, detailing the emotions surrounding it, often leads to new insights and lessons learned.

Articulating our hopes, dreams, concerns, and fears identifies them and helps us discern if these are to be held or discarded. Are they true? Worth the time? Or if false, how do we let them go?

What happens to us is not as important as the meaning we assign to it.
Journaling helps sort this out.
Michael Hyatt

Writing brings light to our life story and fuel to our faith.

Fan the Flame of Listening through our Writing
Reflection Questions:

1. What is your purpose in keeping a journal or writing about your faith?
2. How does writing help you?
3. How could you incorporate writing into your spiritual journey?

Prayer:

Living Word of God, you are the Word. You give us words. Be the ink, the thoughts, the movement behind our pens. Put your hands upon our fingers and let's dance together across the keyboard exploring and igniting our walk of faith with you.

Chapter 5 – The Flame of Worship

In worship, God imparts himself to us.
C.S. Lewis

My assignment for the class was to find an old photograph when I was a child that illustrated part of my life story. I dug into the storage container to find something to share. I had no idea I would find a cherished treasure.

There it was. A black and white, curled in one corner, 3 x 3-inch photo of my dad, holding me as a baby. He is looking at me with such love and protection. Like he was holding a fragile irreplaceable work of art. I don't think I ever recall seeing this pic before. We are face to face, gazing at each other. Slight smiles on both of our faces. Contentment. Love.

The back of the pic revealed another discovery. In his handwriting, Dad wrote a poem/prayer asking the angels to look after me. A gift from a father to his daughter across the years, arriving at just the right moment in time.

The tender beholding of his gaze brought tears to my eyes. I felt loved, held, wanted.

Worship can be a powerful moment of love and acceptance, too.

In worship, we remember who God is and who we are in God. Worship embraces the mystery without words and the wonder beyond imagination. Worship becomes a moment where two hearts beat as one with eyes only on each other. God sees us. We see God. Love exchanged.

Worship is not about us, what we need, or a time to show off our singing or preaching ability. We need to raise our expectation of the gift of worship – our present to God's presence. Worship focuses on God's majesty, his immeasurable greatness with awe, wonder, and reverence.

As I enter worship, whether at home, on retreat, or at a service in my church, I pause and remember the abbreviation MIA.

M – Majesty
I – Immeasurable greatness
A – Awe, wonder and reverence

MIA brings my attention to the great God I am there to worship and takes my eyes from my ego and emotions. Repeating the acronym of MIA reorients our hearts and minds to focus on God and sustains the fire of faith.

> *Awe combined with intimacy is the*
> *essence of Christian worship.*
> *J. D. Grear*

M -Remembering God's Majesty

Worship begins with remembering who God is. We consider his gifts, promises, forgiveness and unbelievable all-encompassing love for us, his creation. Our only response is adoration and praise.

Unable to fully comprehend God's majesty and being, we bow in reverence before God. Worship is for God and we strive to worship the Lord for all that he is and what he has done for us.

Worship begins with the mindset that this moment is about God, not us.

We come to worship with the Lord by getting set, adjusting our mindset, and setting apart our heart to focus only on God.

Getting set involves letting go of our distractions, worries, and cares. Detaching from the human emotions though is not easy. When we see who God is and remember all his gifts, attributes, and glory, we can't help but fall on our knees, humbled and in worship.

Too often I rush into worship distracted by the world and my own agenda. I am learning to pause and take deep breaths as I enter worship. I remind myself who I am about to worship and all the great things he has done. I bring my whole self, my mind, heart, and spirit, into his presence.

Love the Lord your God with all your heart and
with all your soul and with all your mind
and with all your strength.
Mark 12: 30

The physical act of bowing, closing my eyes, looking upward helps my mindset. My heart then is free to be set apart to hear his word, to receive his healing grace, and to be transformed in the fire of his love. My spirit gazes in love, then receives love from God's gaze.

I take a moment to focus on God's attributes. I remember the God who is worthy of our attention, praise, and devotion. I remember his goodness, his promises, and his eternal presence with us.

Wherever we are as worshippers, becomes holy ground.

The Lord reigns, he is robed in majesty;
the Lord is robed in majesty and armed with strength;
indeed, the world is established, firm and secure.
Psalm 93:1

God is above all and worthy of our worship and praise. We see, experience, and know God is more than we can comprehend and great beyond words. When we worship, we are not acting, we react. We respond to God's greatness. Like the photograph of my dad holding me, worship captures a glimpse of heaven that humans normally cannot see.

Our hearts turn and remember the majesty of God, the one who walks with us in the past stories, ours and others, who he is now in the present in his presence, and how he holds our future in his hands. We try, but cannot fully grasp how stunning, how grand, how glorious our God is.

I - Remembering God's Immeasurable Greatness

After we try with our tiny human brains to take in the majesty of God, we come to the reality his greatness is immeasurable. This mystery of God is he is always more, always More.

Worship is our response to the Almighty God, our miniscule offering of love into the never-ending source of all love. With hearts turned to this wonderful God, our egos retreat from trying to be in control and return to its true meager calling of protecting the vulnerable self.

We remember who we are, our sins and mistakes, and we bow before the God of forgiveness and love. We are not God. We are not the center of the universe. Yet God continues to seek us, invites us closer, adopts us as his children, and loves us without restraint.

Remembering God's immeasurable great love and forgiveness brings us into worship. This love from God exceeds our understanding and comprehension. We come as mere humans into the powerful presence of God and leave transformed by his presence, his spirit.

God is spirit, and his worshipers must worship in the Spirit and in truth.
John 4:24

The heat of the Holy Spirit leaves us changed. We humbly approach this immense divine being and bow to his greatness. God's passion for us sets our hearts on fire. God's radiance reflects upon our souls and in our hearts and fuels our faith.

Sometimes we enter worship and can't quite feel God's presence or find the energy to turn our hearts towards him. On rushed Sunday mornings, when kids misbehave or we oversleep, and when troubles steal our attention, how do we focus on God?

I found reading the Sunday scriptures a few days before worship motivates me to center on God. This allows time for the words to prepare me for worship and their meaning settles into my heart and calms my spirit.

During the service, sometimes I simply pray the words of the hymns silently to myself, instead of singing. I look around me to others and pray for them. I gaze at the symbols of God's promises decorating the sanctuary. I listen for key words from the readings or message to remember.

Reciting the words, "Be still and know I am God" brings me into worship.

Simple steps bring my heart focus back on God.

> *We have not worshipped the Lord*
> *until Spirit touches spirit.*
> **Richard Foster.**

A -Remembering God with Awe and Wonder

> **Look at God**
> **Looking at you …**
> **And smiling.**
> **Anthony De Mello**

When our spirit touches God's spirit in worship, the spark of awe and wonder ignite. Our only reaction is praise and adoration. We hear the psalms in new ways. Our songs reverberate deep in our hearts.

Wonder encourages us to stand humbly
before the unfathomable mysteries of human life,
trusting that, in them, we encounter God.
Melanie Svoboda

The original meaning of the word "awe", is *"fear, terror, reverence."* Awe is holy terror of a magnificent God. The word terror certainly carries new meaning for us in the 21st century, but with God there is no fear, alarm, nor panic.

Fear of God is to stand in awe and wonder of the divine. This is not dreadful fear of a tormentor or dangerous authority figure, but a respectful, healthy worship and reverence for a father in heaven who loves us as we are.

Remembering God and plunging into the freedom of his majesty and immeasurable greatness, reminds us we are sharing in something better than us, beyond us.

Awe prompts us not to cheapen God or diminish his glory or his work. We draw near God on holy ground. This is not an ordinary moment nor an ordinary God. This. Is. God. And we worship him.

Don't miss the awe of worship. This wonder intensifies the fire of faith.

At the back of our brains, so to speak, there was a
forgotten blaze or burst of astonishment at our own
existence.
The object of the artistic and spirited life was to dig for
this submerged sunrise of wonder.
G. K. Chesterton

How Worship Fuels our Faith

Faith hears the inaudible, sees the invisible,
believes the incredible,
and receives the impossible.
Unknown

The ingredient of MIA acts like propellant for the fire of
our faith. God's spirit and love stokes the embers of spirit
and love within us. Worship helps us see outside of
ourselves and bow before Someone majestic.

Someone greater than us transforms our heart and will
and thrusts us to do greater things. Worship transforms
into a two-way response. We bring our hearts to the act of
worship and God's love enters us with healing, strength,
and encouragement.

Worship awakens our spirit. We empty ourselves before
the Lord, approaching him humbly and with amazement,
and he showers us with love.

How can we not worship God?

My whole heart I lay upon the altar of the praise, an
whole burnt-offering of praise I offer to thee...Let the
flame of thy love...set on fire my whole heart, let
naught in me be left to myself, naught wherein I may
look to myself, but may I wholly burn towards thee,
wholly be on fire toward thee, wholly love thee, as
though set on fire by thee.
St. Augustine

Fan the Flame of Worship and Reflection Questions

1. Write out your definition of worship and its ingredients for you.
2. Reread the last quote by St Augustine. Rewrite the quote in your own words as a prayer. What does this mean for you? How do these words affect your worship?
3. When you think of God's majesty, what comes to mind?

Prayer

Almighty Lord, you are mystery and wonder and we bow down before you, praising your name as we are overcome with thankfulness for your love. Set our hearts on fire for more of you and transform us as you will. We bow before you as you are our God.

Chapter 6 – The Flame of Service

We make a living by what we get,
but we make a life by what we give.
Winston Churchill

I was burned out. I served as the county health commissioner for 16 years, which meant I suprervised and provided leadership for all the administrative decisions, conflicts, and challenges of a diverse department.

I began this chapter of my life fully believing God wanted me to serve there. The work matched my gifts and I loved public health and making a difference in the lives of my community.

But the problems with personnel, budget, and ever-changing regulations tired me out. I felt more like a fire department, always on call and putting out urgent fires rather than being creative and transformational. Restless, drained, and spent, I yearned for some new type of work, a new calling. I struggled with the lack of motivation and focus to identify where God was leading me.

On top of this, my personal life transitioned. I entered the middle age of life and experienced an empty nest at the same time.

I prayed. I waited impatiently. I tried to force a few things which thankfully didn't work. I journaled, writing out my hopes and frustrations, searching for clarity. I talked with my spiritual director digging for God's wisdom and guidance. This period of my life was dark, confusing, and depressing.

God knew the right timing. I heard about a program offered for lay ministry within our denomination. I prayed and felt God inviting me to explore this avenue. I talked with my pastor and researched the path of study. For the first time in several years, I felt excited about all I could learn and the hope of new possibilities.

One major hurdle loomed before me. I had to be approved by the state candidacy committee. the same rigorous applications required for those being ordained. Paperwork, more paperwork, and even more documentation. Then before officially being accepted to start the learning process, I was required to attend a three-day psychological evaluation.

My family joked I would go to Columbus to be assessed and never return. They would lock me up for sure. But laughing, I still went for the assessment.

We were part of a small group of seven, all discerning various ministry positions. They had us introduce ourselves. I am sure they were observing how we interacted with other people. We filled out personality tests. We talked one on one with a psychologist. We discussed and shared our goals and expectations.

I was nervous, dreading my final appointment with the psychologist to get the results. Fidgeting with my papers, he asked me the question I knew would eventually arrive. Why change when you have a meaningful career now?

I told him about the stress of my current job. My restlessness. I expressed my guilt about no longer making the best of this wonderful opportunity God had given me in a health career.

We reviewed my assessment. And I bravely asked him if I was nuts to start something new like this in midlife.

I have never forgotten his response.

"No, you aren't nuts," he kindly said. "Yes, the gifts you have are very appropriate for the health commissioner work you do.

"I think though, you have other gifts that are asking to be used and the ones you are using right now are overused. The invitation is to balance your gifts in serving."

His words gave me permission to move on. It was okay to let go of what I always thought was where I was to serve and to seek new arenas. The time had arrived to pay attention to the gifts that were dormant and give them room in the garden of my soul to sprout new life.

> *Our life is to be like a river, not a reservoir.*
> *Unknown*

The flame of service burns the brightest with the balanced blending of gifts.

To discover this right mix requires the alignment of our stewardship set, our strength set, our mindset, and our heart set.

Stewardship Set

> *Stewardship is partnership with God.*
> *Unknown*

What does stewardship mean and how can we apply it to service?

The word *"stewardship"* originates in England in the Middle Ages. A manager of a large household was called the steward and his work, the stewardship, implied the oversight and careful responsibility of duties.

Stewardship evolved to also include the concept of caring for something worth preserving and protecting.

God gives us gifts. We are called to be the stewards of those gifts and use them in acts of service for his kingdom. We have a choice. We can ignore or refuse to use those gifts for God or take inventory, pray, and obey.

If two angels were to receive at the same moment a commission from God, one to go down and rule earth's grandest empire, the other to go and sweep the streets of its meanest village, it would be a matter of entire indifference to each which service fell to his lot, the post of ruler or the post of scavenger;
for the joy of the angels lies
only in obedience to God's will.
John Newton

Stewardship is not more to do or to give till we can't do or give anymore. Stewardship is the answer to God's call to obey.

We are motivated by God's love, gratitude for life and his guidance, and like the angels in the quote, to participate in the pure joy of coming alongside God in his work.

Jesus is the perfect servant and the role model for us to follow. We are invited to be stewards in God' kingdom and as we serve, learn to love as Christ loves.

Strength set

All too often we regard stewardship simply as a matter of our giving to God, but this aspect is secondary.
Before we can give, we must possess, and before we possess we must receive.
Therefore, stewardship is, in the first place, receiving God's good and bounteous gifts.
And once received, those gifts are not to be used solely for our own good. They must also be used for the benefit of others,
and ultimately for the glory of God the giver.
The steward needs an open hand to receive from God and then an active hand to give to God and to others.
Murray J. Harris

What are your spiritual gifts? What skills and talents has God planted inside you waiting to grow and bear fruit?

One of life's greatest adventures is the internal work of knowing your true self.

The assessment I took in Columbus before beginning the lay ministry program gave me a glimpse into my strength set.

The psychologists used different tools, such as the Myers-Briggs assessment, the Enneagram, and a spiritual gift inventory. Many books are available to explore our personality and gifts.

I hold the results of these kinds of tests lightly and in prayer. Don't make quick decisions based on one-time results. Talk with others. Pray. Journal. Explore if you feel the description is accurate and if it fits you.

Knowing your strengths and gifts helps to discern where you are going and where to use your talents in a balanced way. I find it easier to let go of ideas that no longer fit and find the courage to explore new possibilities when I take these assessments.

Don't forget your own insight into your life. You know yourself better than others. Think about what you wanted to do as a child. Maybe you wanted to be a professional baseball player. That may not be realistic now, but what insight does that give you? Spend some time exploring your early dreams and desires.

As a child, I wanted to be a writer but felt God leading me into nursing as a teenager. I know nursing was the right field of service for me as an adult, but as I became restless and burned out, a new chapter of life beckoned. I praise God now that he has opened doors for me to come full circle as I use that buried dream from my childhood of writing as a gift blossoming in the second half of life.

Hide not your talents, they for use were made. What's a sundial in the shade?
Benjamin Franklin

Mindset

I've learned that you shouldn't go through life with a catcher's mitt on both hands. You need to be able to throw something back.
Maya Angelou

I love the image of Maya Angelou's catcher's mitt. Holding that picture in my mind creates a powerful vision to motivate service as an opportunity to "throw something back" into the world.

Serving others is more than our job, our duty, what we are labeled and how we are paid. As Richard Foster writes in his book Celebration of Discipline, "*It is one thing to act like a servant; it is quite another to be a servant.*"

Foster brings to light different aspects to serve in practical ordinary ways. His suggestions start with the attitude of seeing and helping others with a new frame of mind:

- The service of hiddenness. Cultivate serving without being known and without the need to be recognized or praised for your giving.

- The service of small things. "Large tasks require great sacrifice for a moment; small things require constant sacrifice." Often the strongest service to others is simple, singular, and small.

- The service of guarding the reputation of others. Foster writes, "The discipline in holding one's tongue works wonders within us."

- The service of common courtesy. Saying please and thank you. Holding the door for someone. Waiting patiently.

- The service of listening. Many times, we don't listen with our full attention; our mind is formulating our response. The gift of listening, being fully present to another is priceless, and begins with aligning our mindset with intention.

We can serve in many ways, big and small, but the awareness starts with our mind, is fueled by the love and compassion from our heart and proceeds with strength and kindness from our hands.

Heart set

> *You can give without loving,*
> *but you cannot love without giving.*
> *Amy Carmichael*

What is your season of life? Is it time to leave the old behind and try new adventure? There are times when the reality of bills, responsibilities, and commitments prevent us from trying a new gift. But seasons come and go and new opportunities surface if we are willing to let go, listen to our heart, and take the risk.

While working as health commissioner, I took the ministry classes, trained to be a spiritual director, and attended writer conferences. I explored and learned, laying the groundwork when I could leave one position to create new avenues to use my gifts. I wasn't sure where this searching would lead, but I took the chance and opportunity to discover.

When the kids were younger the time wasn't right, but as they became more independent, I began to explore different ways to serve. I had a little more time in this season of life to consider possibilities. I took those personality tests. I studied and learned. I listened to ideas from God and from others.

Most importantly, I listened to my heart. Deep in my core, where did I think God was leading me? What excited me and increased my pulse? What stirred my interest? What arena did I keep returning, thirsting for knowing more? Where could I give my best back to God while helping others?

The inner work of the heart takes time and courage.

God will give us patience to wait and strength to cultivate new skills. He will provide the courage to be open and vulnerable as we explore fresh ways of seeing ourselves.

When service matches the heart, the outcome swells the heightened flame of faith.

God wants us to be whole and healthy servants. Servanthood arises from being aligned with God's will and serving with our heart, mind, and soul. This wholeness provides the energy to learn and do. We feel our best when serving from a complete foundation which starts with God and from the heart.

> *Don't just do what you have to do to get by, but work heartily, as Christ's servants doing what God wants you to do. And work with a smile on your face, always keeping in mind that no matter who happens to be giving the orders, you're really serving God.*
> *Ephesians 6:6*

God created us and gave us gifts. When he sends us to live this human life on earth, part of our journey involves discovering our core identity as beloved children of God and learning lessons, such as when to let go and move onward in his service.

Be who God meant you to be and you will set the world on fire.
Catherine of Sienna

When our hearts burn with God's love first, compassion for others ignites.

Whatever you do, work at it with all your heart, as working for the Lord, not for men, since you know that you will receive an inheritance from the Lord as a reward.
It is the Lord Christ you are serving.
Colossians 3:23-24

Fan the Flame of Service Reflection Questions

1. Write out a list of your gifts and talents.
2. How are you using your gifts for the Lord's work?
3. Are there neglected gifts within you buried underneath obligations and busyness that are calling out to grow?
4. Ask God to help you discover where he is leading you as a servant and open your eyes to areas of growth awaiting your next season in life.

Prayer:

God of all gifts, thank you for all you have given us. May we use the skills, interests, and abilities you placed inside our souls in your service.

Chapter 7 - The Flame of Community

The Christian community is not a closed circle of people embracing each other,
but a forward moving group of companions bound together
by the same voice asking for their attention.
Henri Nouwen

Whether we are introverts or the life of the party, we live in community.

One of the strongest basic human needs is the need to belong. We find community in a variety of ways, such as work settings, church, social gatherings, and one on one conversations.

We discover community in small group settings. Community appears in the deep sharing and intimate conversations with a close companion. We experience community when learning in a class or sitting quietly by ourselves in a huge praise-filled church. Community is found in both large and small places.

I discovered an unexpected answer when analyzing a survey from my blog readers. I asked them what spirituality elements would they most like to learn? Several expected topics were mentioned, such as prayer and finding God in daily living, but the answer surprising me the most was the desire to learn more about how to build and experience community.

Community is a hunger, a longing in our society. I sense this yearning to belong intensifying in this century. Our connections with one another are fractured. We feel we can't talk to one another without offending someone. An undertone of suspicion and mistrust invades our communication.

We search to satisfy this longing amid today's rapid changes and growing diversity and globalization. The reality is we won't be going back to "old ways" where church was the center of all activities and we were homogenous in work, ethics, and beliefs. Those old wine skins no longer fit.

We miss community and its gifts of acceptance and understanding one another. Community is a place to learn and thrive and not feel awkward in trying to figure out this thing we call life. Community provides space to explore, discover, and feel safe.

God created the first man, Adam and gave him work to do. He established a protective, life-giving space for man to live. But soon God knew man needed more.

> *The Lord God said, "It is not good for the man to be alone.*
> *I will make a helper suitable for him."*
> *Genesis 2: 18*

God created us for and in community.

Even better, God longs to be with us in community. He loves to walk with us in our lives and be with us as we gather together. God loves community.

I understand the need to belong. I see the necessity of community, but the introvert inside of me squirms. Too many people drain my energy. People can be difficult. I know from personal experience people can hurt. I feel vulnerable so I run from community even though I need its energy and wisdom.

How do we do community in a healthy way? How can we discover our story within other people's story all within God's story?

All good fires need combustible materials to fuel the flame. In community, adding the elements of sharing, knowing, and listening ease us closer to joining others around the fire of faith. Some of us who are more uncomfortable in communities can apply these ingredients to our own faith and interactions.

Sharing

How do we build bridges between one another to create strong communities?

One of the first steps is the act of sharing. We share our stories and get to know one another's backgrounds. We gain understanding about how each other think, we share what we believe, and why we are passionate about what we do. This knowledge gives us greater understanding and acceptance.

Within your own communities, talk about your shared Christian roots and identity. I have the rich experience this year of helping to plan our local congregation's 150th anniversary. Seeing the old photos. Learning the stories from our shared history. Reminiscing about former pastors and youth group antics. All these memories unite those of us on the committee with fresh connections.

I love our church's adult Sunday School. Though not many people attend, our small group has developed a sense of walking with one another through life's ups and downs. We participate in a trusting environment where we are missed if we don't come and feel comfortable expressing doubts, fears, and confusions. We continue to grow, learn, and explore more about God with one another.

Community hurts, too. When we allow ourselves to be open to love and sharing, we are also vulnerable to misunderstandings, judgments, and wounds. We intentionally work to provide safe environments and boundaries to prevent or ease the downside of community. Since we were created for community, we need to identify behaviors that build up others, not harm them.

Community, when people feel safe, can be a place where forgiveness surfaces, hurts heal, and fractures mend. When we remember God's free grace is for all of us, we learn to offer that grace to one another.

Though this practice is not easy and our egos resist it, when we honor one another, we honor God. We hold a shared ministry of loving and accepting each other as children of God.

Communities also grow stronger when we gather regularly, building positive connections as we do things together, and share ideas and resources. Communities then generate nourishment for our souls in new ways. Participating in a variety of simple things together gives us chances to connect with others, build trust, and get involved in doing things together.

Our stories entwine with one another with roots deep in God's love. The act of sharing affirms and builds these bridges leading to the sense of belonging. Community becomes grounded in the word "we" and less in the word, "they."

Friendship is born at that moment when one man says to another:
"What! You too? I thought I was the only one."
C.S. Lewis

Knowing

I learned the hard way the importance of knowing another person while building community. When I didn't know and understand a co-worker, our communication and connection with one another failed.

Early in my health career, our place of employment divided into two opposing camps. The previous director left, fracturing those of us loyal to her versus those who wanted her out of her position.

I cried every day going to work. The tension in the office rocketed even more because several of us shared office space. Often more was said in the strained silence than in our curt conversations.

One lady drove me crazy. She always criticized me, highlighting my faults.

I asked God for help. I even expressed the words "Lord, take this thorn from my side." Of course, I was referring to my obstinate office mate.

I know I said that prayer for several days when I heard God's whisper *"Maybe you are a thorn in her side."*

Ouch. I didn't want to hear that message. I wanted to be right. The truth of the situation was, though, I was as much at fault in the relationship as she was.

I began to pray for her. I considered her situation. She was a single mother, raising two teenagers. I saw her in a new light as a devoted nurse who wanted to do a good job and loved what she did.

My heart softened towards her when I began to know her story better.

Tensions slowly eased. I know my change in attitude helped but the healing occurred the most when we communicated as a team, not as rivals. We began to hear each other. A new respect for each other's opinions emerged. We never became close friends, but we could work side by side with each other.

Where only thorns once grew, flowers began to grow.

Everyone has a story to tell. Everyone's story gives the other person insight to our own actions, behaviors, and thoughts. God lives within everyone's story if we only take the time to see his presence in another person.

A good start to knowing others is to learn their story. Let your guard down and share your story. What are the defining moments in your life? How did you get to know God? When do you experience his presence? What is unique in your life's journey and your quest to know and follow God?

When we know our own spiritual autobiography and listen to other people's narrative, we discover their strengths and build relationships.

Knowing another person takes time, openness, and a willingness to listen. We begin to relate to one another on a deeper level. Once we understand others, compassion and community grows.

> *Seek first to understand, then to be understood.*
> **Steven Covey**

Listening

The gift of listening to another is priceless and rare. The other person often doesn't need to be fixed or to hear the blah-blah-blah of advice. They just need to be heard.

> *If you're like most people, you probably seek first to be understood; you want to get your point across. And in doing so, you may ignore the other person completely, pretend that you're listening,*
> *selectively hear only certain parts of the conversation or attentively focus on only the words being said, but miss the meaning entirely.*
> *So why does this happen?*
> *Because most people listen with the intent to reply, not to understand.*
> *You listen to yourself as you prepare in your mind what you are going to say,*
> *the questions you are going to ask, etc.*
> *You filter everything you hear through your life experiences, your frame of reference.*
> *You check what you hear against your autobiography and see how it measures up.*

And consequently, you decide prematurely what the
other person means
before he/she finishes communicating.
Steven Covey

How can we listen better?

- The answer is in the word "listen." Mix up the letters and you discover its secret: *silent*.

- To listen to another is to be silent. Quiet your next words. Hush your mind. Still your heart and just listen.

- Ask God to help you listen more attentively.

- Pay attention to what is being said and what is not being expressed.

- Be open and accepting, not judging.

- Ask questions to clarify and to help you identify the emotion behind the story.

- Practice. Practice. Practice.

Hearing another person deeply fosters intimacy, friendship, and community. We share in their journey and know them better. We come alongside them as we walk together through life.

We share joys and troubles. We help the other person and share space and resources. We bond with mutual values. We spend time with one another listening, sharing, laughing, and crying. We accept each other's stories and learn to understand each other's points of view.

Building community takes time to nurture the relationship, courage to be vulnerable, and trust to grow love and compassion.

Common ground is the strong foundation for building community. Community fortifies the flame of faith.

Fan the Flames of Community Reflection Questions

1. Who could you reach out to build community?
2. Write out your spiritual story and spend time listening with others to learn their story.
3. Practice deep listening. What did you notice about how you listen? How can you improve?

Prayer

Creator Lord, you made us to live and thrive in community. Give us the wisdom to build relationship through sharing, knowing, and listening to your children. Help us see others through your eyes of love.

Chapter 8 - The Flame of Letting Go

We must be willing to let go of the life we've planned,
so as to have the life that is waiting for us.
Joseph Campbell

I moved to a new school in 6th grade. I was scared. I was alone. I was fat.

The most wonderful gift of this new adventure was meeting Chrissy who became and still is my "sister" and lifelong friend.

The worst gift from this new adventure was the boy who sat behind me, laughing, and calling me "fatso."

I still feel the sting of his words, but Chrissy gave me love and acceptance. Her voice rings in my heart today, right next to that boy's voice.

You would think after decades I could let go of negative nicknames from childhood. I carry other burdens too, such as the deaths of loved ones, rejection from people I thought were friends, failures and embarrassments emptying my confidence.

Past personal disasters and adversities often shape our identity. Bruises and scars to our ego form our behaviors and decisions. We cause some of our own misfortunes, while other messes descend upon our lives uninvited.

Wounds and hurts impact what we think of ourselves and how we act with others. How we were treated molds our expectations and influences our thinking. Too often fear, worry, and preconceived notions govern our hearts.

Who has the power in our lives? Is it fear? Do we continue to cling tightly to our past experiences and what others told us about ourselves and our value? Can we empty our hands so we are free to reach out and embrace future possibilities? Where is our belief in God in this tension of holding fast versus letting go?

The practice of letting go creates the space for the flames of our faith to expand and light our lives and the lives of others.

When Fear Rules in Our Hearts

I am a person who likes to control. I want to know what is going to happen and when. I am comfortable in my knowledge of who fits in which box and prefer the black and white patterns of predictability.

But through the years I've learned this: control arises from fear.

We learn fear when we experience being hurt. We sense danger when we feel vulnerable. The little child within us quivers with the unknown and when we step into the arena where we have no control.

Fear can be beneficial when it teaches us to be cautious in certain circumstances. Fear protects our ego and at times even our lives. The fear of a possible car crash reminds me to buckle my seatbelt.

Fear is a powerful emotion and one that influences more than we realize. Fear paralyzes and can overwhelm us with a sense of helplessness and even rage.

Fear has its place, but not in control of all our decisions. Fear is a tool to use when appropriate, but don't allow fear to have all the power in determining life's course.

When I let go of what I am, I become what I might be.
When I let go of what I have, I receive what I need.
Lao Tzu

How do we let go of fear's control over us?

The first step is awareness that fear is influencing our decisions and behaviors. Name the emotion you experience. Think about why fear surfaced now. Listen to your self-talk and analyze what is true and how fear hampers your progress or blocks a solution.

I use a silly visual to help me let go of fear. I stop and take several deep breaths. Then I tell fear thanks for being here, but get out of the driver's seat and enjoy the ride in the back seat. God is determining the direction of my car. He is in control.

> *There are things that we never want to let go of, people we never want to leave behind. But keep in mind that letting go isn't the end of the world, it's the beginning of a new life.*
> *Unknown*

When Clinging Tightly Rules in our Hearts

> *You can clutch the past so tightly to your chest that it leaves your arms too full to embrace the present.*
> *Jan Glidewell*

Our ego naturally defines itself by past experiences. Whether good or bad, the stories we tell ourselves and the voices of the world we listen to influence our hearts.

We cling to past beliefs, images from childhood, and wounds from hurts, nicknames, and cruel incidences. We don't stop to consider other options since from our point of view, this is all we know.

Letting go is difficult. The openness of no longer fitting our self-identity in a clean box with defined borders produces moments of panic in us. We stand vulnerable, naked before the world, not sure who we are and where we are to go.

When I retired from health care and entered the writing and speaking ministries, I felt like I was 14 years old amid a teenager's identity crisis. I no longer held a job that defined me and at the same time my children began their lives as adults. My ego laid exposed, raw, and unguarded.

Being the "boss" formed my identity. Letting go of that position, I lost my sense of self I had to learn to let go of the old self and embrace the new person I was becoming, grounded in knowing she was a beloved child of God.

Another time I wrote unexpectedly in my journal about my image of God. I realized when I thought of God, I imagined an old man sitting on the far, unreachable side of a room. I smiled remembering he looked like the first minister from my childhood. Knowing that I could release that image as no longer true. I began to explore all the attributes of God and to get know him better in his many facets. The image of God as savior, guide, and friend transformed me.

When I was a child, I talked like a child, I thought like a child, I reasoned like a child. When I became a man, I put the ways of childhood behind me
I Corinthians 13: 11

Clinging to the past, to images that no longer work, and to stories that are not true, prevent us from accepting all the promised blessings from God. What burdens are you holding onto too tightly?

Holding on is believing that there's only a past; letting go is knowing that there's a future.
Daphne Rose Kingman

When God Rules in our Hearts

When God rules in our hearts, we acknowledge only God is in control. This helps us let go of hurts, worries, and burdens. Reminding myself of his promises and how God remains with me, I release my grip on the past and the things I need to relinquish.

I still hear that boy from sixth grade mocking me and calling me names. I know some pain will never be forgotten and some scars are permanent, but they don't determine my value or direction in life.

Only God does.

God invites us beyond our fear into faith.

Knowing we can live as our true selves as the beloved children of God frees us to explore God's opportunities. When our hearts are not weighed down with burdens, we learn to trust in God.

God is in charge and gives us ideas for releasing of fear and welcoming his sovereignty.

One method of letting go is to walk a labyrinth. When you walk the concentric path of a labyrinth, you slowly release the weights of the world. The slow pace, winding path that mirrors life's journey, and the relaxing benefits of this practice almost rock us into the comforting arms of God.

Following the path, you lose sight and expectations of seeing what is ahead and you focus on one step at a time. We trust in the journey and the One who walks with us.

Another way to let go is to attend a multi-day retreat. The silence and solitude of spending time with God at a retreat center brings healing, strength, and listening. We hear God, know his presence, and surrender to him.

On one summer retreat, I stood by a cold burnt bonfire in the middle of a meadow. I symbolically threw my past images, my wounds, my troubles into God's fire. I still have on my desk and can see it as I write this, a blackened ember from that fire where I submitted to God's sovereignty and control.

Some people find the practice of fasting beneficial. Emptying ourselves of an impulse, habit, or obsession is another form of recognizing God ruling in our heart. We acknowledge what is coming between us and God and what pulls us away from him. Often, we listen to those false voices, the fears that hold us back and the stories we were told instead of turning to God.

Fasting is important in Christian experience because it deepens within the whole self a sense of one's dependence upon the strength of God. Fasting is more than an act of abstinence. It is an affirmation act; it is a way of waiting on God; it is an act of surrender.
James Earl Massey

Fasting creates space for God to heal us and the stillness to hear his voice of love. Fasting strips away the false beliefs we cling to and opens our hands to receive God's presence.

St. Augustine once said that God is always trying to give good things to us, but our hands are too full to receive them. If our hands are full, they are full of the things to which we are addicted. And not only our hands but also our hearts, minds, and attention are clogged with addiction. Our addictions fill up the spaces within us, space where grace might flow.
Gerald May

Letting go allows God to enter our hearts and breathe his breath of life and forgiveness onto our fire of faith.

Fan the Flame of Letting Go Reflection Questions

1. Name what you need to release.
2. What from the past do you cling to and may be called to let go of?

3. What practices have helped you in the past or could you try now to release fear and welcoming God's sovereignty in your life?

Prayer

God, you are in control. We lay before you our past, our fears, our burdens. We ask you to heal our wounds with your love and direct our ways with your presence. You are our ruler – the one who sets us free. Thank you for your strength, wisdom, and guidance through the challenging practice of letting go.

Chapter 9 – The Flame of Adventures with God

To fall in love with God is the greatest romance;
to seek him the greatest adventure;
to find him, the greatest human achievement.
St Augustine

******

At first I saw God as an observer, maybe someone with a telescope who watched me from far away. He was like a judge, keeping track of what I did right and what I did wrong. At the end of my life he would decide whether I deserved heaven or hell. I did not know God back then.

But later on, I met Jesus, and I started to see life like a bike ride. It was a tandem bike and now Jesus was in the back helping me to pedal. I don't know just when he suggested that we switch places, but life has not been the same since. When I had control I knew what way I wanted to go. It was a little boring but predictable. I had the same friends, we did the same things. Life was the shortest distance between two points.

But when he took the lead, he showed me delightful long cuts, up mountains and through rocky places at break-neck speed. It was all I could do to hang on! Even though sometimes it all seemed crazy, he'd just keep saying "pedal."

I would become worried and ask: "Where are you taking me? Can I trust you?" But He'd just laugh and say: "Yes," and slowly I started to trust. I forgot my boring life and entered into the adventure. And when I'd say I'm scared he'd lean back and take my hand. He took me to meet people I never thought I would ever associate with and they became my friends. They had things that I needed… gifts of acceptance and joy, lessons about life and love. And sometimes we'd meet people who needed a gift from me. I'd never done that before. When I would be overwhelmed by it all, Jesus would just smile and say: "I told you it would be fun!"

I must say I did not trust him at first in control of my life. I thought he would wreck it. But he knows bike secrets, and I have learned that they are the secrets to life too. He knows how to take sharp corners, how to jump high rocks and how to stop and rest in the most amazing places. Now I am just learning to enjoy being with my Lord, to pedal without fear in the strangest and most beautiful places, to enjoy the wind in my hair and the sun on my face. I could never have gone where I have gone, or seen what I have seen, or become what I have become without him. And still he just says: Pedal.
Anonymous

I love this story. I smile every time I read the line: "*I don't know just when he suggested that we switch places, but life has not been the same since.*" So true. Welcome to the adventure of following God.

Thinking of our life with God in the framework of adventure loosens my need to control and makes approaching all kinds of circumstances more fun and filled with hope and light. I know Who is leading the way and am slowly learning to trust his path.

On this wild, exciting exploration with God, we get to know our Guide in new ways. We don't worry as much about the details, trusting he will work things out when the time is right. We enjoy the travel and the process more than the how and when of reaching our destination.

When God takes the lead, we journey to places we never considered, cross paths with people our safer route would never find and grow and stretch our mind and faith in powerful fresh ways.

The word "*adventure*" derives from Latin and means "*A thing about to happen*." Though the word may be associated with concepts of unknown perils and excitement, in the 13th century adventure also meant, "*a wonder, a miracle; and an account of marvelous things.*"

Seeing God as leading the way on a tandem bike creates a delightful limitless image of life.

The symbol of the tandem bike also implies we do need to do some work. We need to pedal, following God's lead and patterns. We follow God and together set out to explore new places.

How do we learn to enjoy and not resist the adventure of God?

When we name our longings, tame our ego, and remain with God, our final story blazes with God's love, grace, and delight. Grab that bike and join God on his adventure.

Naming our Longings

> **Desire helps us find our way. But we first have to know them.**
> **The deep longings of our hearts are our holy desires.**
> **Not only desires for physical healing, but also the desires for change, for growth, for a fuller life. Our deepest desires, those desires that lead us to become who we are, are God's desires for us.**
> **They are ways that God speaks to you directly.**
> **Desire is a key part of spirituality because desire is a key way that God's voice is heard in our lives.**
> **And our deepest desire, planted within us, is our desire for God.**
> **James Martin**

Most of us want to follow God more closely and let him lead the way in our lives. Sorting through our conflicting distractions and desires that take us away from God's path becomes the challenge.

How do we know the desire God planted in our hearts? Are we on the right adventure with God?

The practice of naming our longings takes time and inner work, but will lead to clarity. Once identified, this core desire serves as a light on our path and a touchstone so we don't stray.

Longings drive our behaviors. Cravings and motivation rise from our human survival instinct. We see something. We want that item. We feel restless and "hunt" for the answers to our unclear desires.

Our longings are the echoes from the empty chambers of our heart.

In the late afternoon, I "graze" through the kitchen cupboards, not knowing what I am hungry for, but focused on finding, tasting, filling some hunger inside me. The sweet chocolate or salty chips taste good for a few seconds, but don't satisfy my real need. My body usually needs water or rest, not wasted calories.

Our hearts too are empty. We stuff them with work, sports, hobbies, food, alcohol, busyness, but none of that quenches our thirst.

The expression used frequently for our deepest desires is a "God-shaped hole in everyone's heart." The origin of this phrase comes from Blaise Pascal from this quote:

> *What else does this craving, and this helplessness, proclaim but that there was once in man a true happiness, of which all that now remains is the empty print and trace?*
> *This he tries in vain to fill with everything around him, seeking in things that are not there the help he cannot find in those that are, though none can help, since this*

*infinite abyss can be filled only with an infinite and immutable object;
in other words by God himself.*

The hollow within us waits for the holy. We are hungry for the one who created us, loves us and who wants to be with us. God calls us back to him.

God wants us to clarify and articulate our hopes and dreams and share them with him. I found what helps me most is to write out what I am desiring about my relationship with God.

I begin with prayer. I ask God for his guidance. I write, stumbling over words that don't fit at first. I open the thesaurus to find another way of expressing my ache for God. I look up Bible verses and scan inspirational quotes for snippets of wisdom.

I write and write again, revising, praying, working on a sentence or two that names my desire for God.

I take my journal with these scribblings on retreat and listen for his voice. What new words bubble up? Sometimes I will be listening to a podcast or a sermon and a few words will drip from heaven into my heart.

With honesty, I tell God how I feel and describe where I am stuck. As I struggle to explain in writing my images, words, and thoughts and dig deeper to express my inner longings, I experience the presence of God.

Here are examples I wrote over the past few years naming my deepest longing:

"Visible and invisible Radiance; I desire to dwell and indwell in the enormity of God."

"Let me dwell in your echo forever, Lord."

"I want to continue discerning what draws me closer to God and let go what doesn't."

"To live a life of prayer and an echo/reflection of your love.
To live open to your transforming love.
To let go and be immersed in your lavish love.
To be pliable in your creative love,
and to be one with your amazing love."

These prayers are a work in progress; probably a lifelong unfolding of my inner desire for God.

God wants us to ask and identify this core hunger for him. When we spend time with him listening, the image will emerge.

We all know the story of how a caterpillar evolves to its true destination of a beautiful butterfly. But we forget the time spent in the cocoon, where he rests, waits, and dissolves into emptiness. Then the butterfly struggles, grapples, and wriggles his way into new creation. The work within, though hard and dark, leads to life.

Trust in the Lord and do good; dwell in the land and enjoy safe pasture. Delight yourself in the Lord and he will give you the desires of your heart. Commit your way to the Lord; trust in him and he will do this: He will make your righteousness shine like the dawn, the justice of your cause like the noonday sun. Be still before the Lord and wait patiently for him.
Psalm 37: 5-7

Our prayer starts with the desire to love and know God and let him lead the way. Be honest with all our hopes, dreams, hurts and battles and bring them to God. Do the inner work.

What is your deepest desire in your relationship with God? Delight yourself in the Lord. Take that bike ride.

Taming the Ego

I find it hard to admit I am not in control. I like to think I have my act together, my plans clear and in place, and that I know what I am doing. Quite a mask, isn't it?

Knowing I am not in control is and will continue to be a lifelong lesson for me. How about you?

When I frame my life as an adventure with God, I relinquish my sense of control to him.

We still need our egos. They protect us. They are part of who we are. They give us a sense of self, but they shouldn't be in the driver's seat. God is. They can ride in the back seat. Come along, ego, but know your place.

God guides the tandem bike; my job is to pedal.

One of my key spiritual practices is attending an annual silent retreat. Recently I registered for the four days of solitude and quiet with God and received the confirmation with details of the event.

All looked like what I expected until I noticed they were offering something new this time. Each evening we would meet with a small group of fellow retreatants to share something we were experiencing during our time with God.

GASP!! Leave my comfortable silence to talk with others? I was already discussing my retreat with a spiritual director each day. Why would I want to share intimate details with strangers?

I was not happy. I was angry, I resisted the change. I stomped my feet like a two-year-old and pouted.

The next morning, I told God I wasn't going to do it. I felt the group interaction violated my quiet time with him. I saw no advantage for me to participate in this activity.

I. I. I. My ego soared into high gear. What's in it for me?

When my words dwindled, I sat quietly with God. Then I heard his whisper. Maybe I would hear him in new ways in the words from someone in that group. I began to wonder if God wanted me there for reasons I could never imagine and maybe never would know.

Ok Lord, you win. Ego, back into place. Let's see where God takes this side trip that I didn't plan for or have control over.

As the retreat ended, I can honestly say that the small group meetings were powerful. I gained insight, not only from feedback from the others about my experience but from listening to what they shared. I felt community and affirmation. Another retreatant shared that my story gave her a fresh awareness of her story.

God knew better than my ego.

This experience reminded me about the commercials for the self-parking cars. They set the car to park and release hands, raising them from controlling the steering wheel. When we take the car through a car wash, again, we move the gear into neutral, foot off the pedal, and hands from the steering wheel.

God's adventures are like these moments. My ego may protest at first. I may hesitate with being uncomfortable or quiver with the *"what if's"* and imaginative terrors that await. In the end, I lift my hands and let God do the steering.

God takes the lead on this wonderful bike ride with him. Interesting that in the original Hebrew language the words *"cease striving"* means letting our hands down.

Taming my ego means I can't steer the tandem bike from the back seat. I let go and let God do the driving.

> *Humble yourselves, therefore, under God's mighty hand, that he may lift you up in due time. Cast all your anxiety on him because he cares for you.*
> *1 Peter 5: 6-7*

Remaining with God

> *Life is not a problem to be solved;*
> *it is an adventure to be lived.*
> *John Eldredge*

What happens when we remain in the second seat? The ride leads us to places and people we may never have encountered on our own. Riding in sync with the Lord brings contentment, peace, and out of this world joy.

Does God control everything in my life? What about free will? The image of letting God lead and the idea of living this adventure with him aligns me in open, clearer communication with him, not a dominating "his way or no way" dictatorship.

When God controls our lives, we start with God first. We take our hopes, dreams, and concerns to him before acting.

A few years back an interesting job offer was presented to me. The job matched my gifts and I prayed about wanting to serve others in a new capacity. Was this the opportunity God wanted for me?

I gathered more information about the job and discussed its aspects with my hubby and with others. I journaled my excitement about the offer and my confusion whether this was my calling. I prayed. I waffled between taking the position and turning it down. My indecisiveness created quite an internal turmoil.

After several days, I felt God saying, "What do you really want?"

Less than a second ticked by when I blurted, "My gut tells me not to do it."

Immediately I felt at peace. I heard God say, "I will bless either way you decided. I want a relationship with you, not a dictatorship."

God in the lead, I follow, pedaling along with him. In this relationship where he takes me places beyond my imagination and on unexpected adventures, we are together. Living a life with God inspires a sacred synergy that goes beyond any simple, dreary life my ego creates.

Framing and remaining in our relationship with God as an adventure helps us draw closer to him as a friend and opens our communication. Our faith grows best with God leading the way.

Fan the Flames of Adventures with God Reflection Questions

1. Write out your deepest desire in your relationship with God.
2. Where is God leading you, coming alongside of you on the adventure of life?
3. When have you heard God in your discerning?

Prayer

Adventurous God, thank you for taking the front seat of our lives and leading us into new places and meeting new people. What an honor it is to be able to come to you with our deepest desires, hopes, and fears, knowing you will hold them gently in your heart and hear them with your spirit. We remain with you, continually receiving nourishment for our faith, as we ride along with you on the great adventure.

Chapter 10 – The Flame of Gratitude

Piglet noticed that even though he had a very small heart,
it could hold a rather large amount of gratitude.
A.A. Milne

Gratitude enlarges our hearts and adds flavor and color to our lives. I believe being thankful protects our heart and mind too. Gratitude fuels our faith.

When I practice gratitude, there is less chance that despair and disillusionment will dig their claws into my spirit. Discouragement seeds won't grow in the heart of a grateful person.

The Practice of Giving Thanks

My experience with intentionally practicing gratitude has been transformational. This spiritual discipline helps me focus on what I have, not the vapor wishes I think I need.

Being thankful helps me step out of the way, thanking God for all things, not relying on my own self-centered strength.

Gratitude teaches me the fun in discovering hidden blessings, treasures I may have missed if I hadn't been paying attention.

Counting my blessings turns what my emotions blindly convey as a rotten day into *"hey that wasn't so bad after all"* type of reflection.

Thankfulness adds meaning to life, even in difficult times.

Gratitude is not only the greatest of virtues, but the
parent of all others.
Cicero

What is Gratitude?

At times our own light goes out and is rekindled by a spark from another person. Each of us has cause to think with deep gratitude of those who have lighted the flame within us.
Albert Schweitzer

Different studies define gratitude with various terms. A good challenge to undertake is to write out your own definition of thankfulness and how you express this in your own life.

You can start by exploring words such as blessings, noticing, acknowledging, abundance, and wonder. Is it learning to live each moment as a gift? Is it reframing our life into God's light and understanding? Is it living in the present moment and not taking things for granted? What are the ingredients of gratefulness?

For many people gratitude is simply the characteristic of being thankful. Gratitude is a state of the mind and the heart when we affirm, notice, and appreciate the little pleasures and huge blessings in life.

Additional elements of gratitude include:

- Recognizing the unearned blessings in life.
- Honoring the presence of gratitude that exists in all people. Every language in the world has a way to express thankfulness.
- Increasing gratitude within us and acknowledging it is a skill that can be cultivated and nourished.
- Savoring the gifts of gratitude, such as generosity, forgiveness, and contentment.

Gratitude can transform common days into thanksgivings,
turn routine jobs into joy,
and change ordinary opportunities into blessings.
Williams Arthur Ward

Reading about the research behind the power of gratitude confirms to me that this spiritual practice is an essential and powerful tool to nourish us in our faith journey. Being grateful is a choice we make that holds vast benefits for the individual and the world.

I wonder how much hate, greed, and distrust would be overcome if there were more gratitude among all people. I can't change the whole world, but I can start with myself and those I touch.

God gives the blessings and we give thanks for the blessings. A cycle of giving and saying thanks leads to true thanksgiving.

> ***Give thanks for a little and you will find a lot.***
> ***David Steindl-Rast***

The Power of Gratitude

Pondering gratitude stirs my curiosity about why is gratitude as a spiritual practice so powerful? This ever-growing field of research is amazing and proves the benefits of gratitude:

- o Gratitude makes you appreciate the value of something, and when you appreciate the value of something, you extract more benefits from it. You are less likely to take life for granted.
- o Studies found if you are grateful, you are less resentful towards someone who has something you don't have.
- o Gratitude helps you recover more quickly from stress, adversity, and trauma by helping you interpret negative events. It has been found to give you a perspective to help guard against post-traumatic stress and lasting anxiety.
- o People who are grateful tend to be more helpful and empathic, more spiritual and religious, more forgiving, and less

materialistic than others who are less predisposed to gratefulness.
- o Gratitude increases our sense of self-worth.
- o People who are thankful score higher in happiness scores on assessment tests.
- o Gratitude improves relationships. Gratitude makes us nicer, more trusting, more social, and more appreciative. As a result, it helps us make more friends, deepen our existing relationships, and improves our marriages.
- o People who practice gratitude consistently report benefits such as stronger immune systems and lower blood pressure, higher levels of positive emotions, more joy, optimism, and happiness. Grateful people act with more generosity and compassion and feel less lonely and isolated.
- o Several studies indicate that keeping a gratitude journal resulted in higher quality sleep.
- o Gratitude reduces feelings of envy, makes our memories happier, increases the experience of good feelings, and helps us bounce back from stress.

How to Harness the Power of Gratitude

- o **Keep a gratitude journal**. This powerful practice changes people's lives when they begin to write down things they are grateful for. The simple habit reframes our perspective, brings us hope, and enables us to seek and find good in life.

Try it right now. Stop reading and make a list five things that make you thankful.
Here is my list:
The sunshine outside my window.
My hardworking, reliable hubby.
How wonderful my kids have grown into as adults and the spouses they married.

Health – able to breathe, move, and wake up every morning.
That God is patient with me and all my quirks, missteps, and sin.

- **Practice Daily Examen**. Once a day, review your day and find at least one item to thank God for from that day. I often fall asleep at night, thanking God. There is no better way to enter sleep than in the cradle of gratitude, being rocked asleep with the hands of God. The key is to notice, then behold all that we have in life. See it all, the big stuff and the simple pleasures.
- **Do something for someone else**. Ever notice when you are upset, discontent, or discouraged when you help someone else, reach out to someone in need, it changes your perception of life completely and lifts your spirit? Serve someone today.
- **Simply say "thank you" more often.**

If the only prayer you say in your life is 'thank you,' that would suffice.
Meister Eckhart

- **Make a list of what you don't have that you can be grateful for**: For example: no ants in the kitchen, no flat tires, and how I can walk without pain (I had a back injury several years ago that made it difficult to walk for at least six months, so I am grateful walking now without pain).
- **Open your eyes and heart and consider what you can be thankful for that may not at first be obvious.** I am thankful for my hubby's snoring at night. I have friends who have lost their husbands and would give almost anything to hear him breathing at night again. I am grateful for when the internet works, the car starts up easily, the microwave heats my coffee up in less than two minutes, that I have work to do, a roof over my

head, the sense of hearing to enjoy my grandkids' giggles, and food in my refrigerator.

- **Blessing or Burden?** I have a friend who has cancer, a cancer that will eventually kill him. He said to me once that he has having difficulty finding the blessing in the gift of cancer. Gift of cancer? Wow! That really lingered with me. We all get "gifts" in life we didn't ask for or want. Just this morning, as I prayed for my friend, God gently told me: the lesson is what the gift tells me about God, that he is always with me, no matter what happens. It reminds me life is fragile and should be cherished. Maybe the blessing is in remembering God is patient with me and the wait is worth it. I unwrapped the gift of knowing deeply that I am a beloved child of God.

- **Gratitude is transformation.** Practice it ~~even when you don't feel thankful,~~ especially when you don't feel thankful. Counting your blessings does work and we can cultivate an attitude of gratitude.

- **Go a day without complaining, whining or being negative.** This practice is harder than you think. One Lent I gave up being sarcastic and found out how deeply those types of words and thoughts dug into my being. I struggled to keep my mouth shut but learned a valuable lesson.

- **Find a trigger reminding you to say thank you.** Every time you pick up a spoon, pass through a doorway, stop at a red light, pause and be thankful. I have my phone set to chirp each day at 3 pm to remind be to be thankful.

- **Share, don't compare.** Focus on what you have right now to share with others. When our eyes pay attention to what others have, we get drawn into the comparison game. Starting with your blessings you hold now and offering them to others creates the better point of view.

- **Savor, don't waver.** When we focus on what we don't have and rush through life without stopping to appreciate all our blessings, we miss opportunities for gratitude. The busyness of life, demands of work, and commitment of family often places our hearts into automatic mode where we begin to take things for granted. We assume the microwave will heat up our tea and the car will turn over, instead of being thankful for these conveniences. Counting our blessings each day switches off the trigger within us between the wavering of not paying attention and the instinct to compare our lives to what others have or appear to have. We fail to appreciate our health, life, job, family until something happens and these gifts are lost. We take too much for granted. Savor God's gift of life.

To be grateful is to recognize the Love of God in everything He has given us — and He has given us everything.

Every breath we draw is a gift of His love, every moment of existence is a grace, for it brings with it immense graces from Him.

Gratitude therefore takes nothing for granted, is never unresponsive, is constantly awakening to new wonder and to praise of the goodness of God.

For the grateful person knows that God is good, not by hearsay but by experience.

And that is what makes all the difference.
Thomas Merton

One practice I use to discover and pay attention to being thankful is using reflective questions. I write these questions in my journal and add them to my daily prayers.

Here are 25 questions I use to nurture gratitude:

1. What am I most grateful for today?

2. Look around you right now where you are. When you pay attention to your environment, what emerges as something to be thankful for?

3. What is the best thing that has happened today?

4. What is the best thing to happen in your life this past week?

5. What is the best thing to happen to you this past year?

6. What is your favorite color and what does it suggest?

7. Think of one or more loved ones and spend a moment being grateful for how they have enriched your life.

8. If you could talk face to face with God right now, how would you thank him?

9. What difficult time has made you stronger?

10. What abilities do you have that you are grateful for?

11. What ordinary blessings, often taken for granted, can you give thanks for? (Such as clean water, electricity, food)

12. What have other people done for you that brings thanks into your life?

13. What person(s) in history because of what they wrote/did invite you to give thanks?

14. What has changed in the past year that you could now give thanks for?

15. What opportunities are now appearing that welcome gratitude?

16. Take a walk and allow what you see and hear become points of gratitude.

17. If you can see, give thanks.

18. If you can hear, say thank you.

19. If you can taste, savor that moment.

20. Take a deep breath and be grateful for life.

21. What do you own that you are grateful for?

22. What trips/vacations bring back memories and lessons that fill you with thankfulness?

23. What ordinary times with friends make you smile and give thanks?

24. Think of someone who is difficult and challenging for you and find something to be grateful for in that relationship.

25. What is something/someone you would miss if they were no longer with you? Give thanks right now for their presence.

You say grace before meals. All right. But I say grace before the concert and the opera, and grace before the play and pantomime, and grace before I open a book, and grace before sketching, painting, swimming, fencing, boxing, walking, playing, dancing and grace before I dip the pen in the ink.
G.K. Chesterton

The powerful practice of gratitude brings our eyes and hearts back to the fire of all of God's blessings in life. We see things we take for granted, moments we missed or neglected to savor and we experience God more deeply in times we thought he was absent.

Let gratitude be the pillow upon which you kneel to say your nightly prayer. And let faith be the bridge you build to overcome evil and welcome good.
Maya Angelou

Gratitude changes us and transforms others. Everything tastes better with gratitude. Spice up your life today and be thankful. Seasoned with gratitude, the flames of faith will grow.

Gratitude unlocks the fullness of life.
It turns what we have into enough, and more.
It turns denial into acceptance,
chaos to order,
confusion to clarity.
It can turn a meal into a feast,
a house into a home,
a stranger into a friend.
Melody Beattie

Fanning the Flame of Gratitude Reflection Questions

1. Think of one or more loved ones and spend a moment being grateful for how they have enriched your life
2. Who has helped you know God and how could you show your gratitude?
3. What is one step you can take today for more gratitude?

Prayer

Lord, we are so thankful for all your gifts. Open our eyes to see your blessings. We bring our hearts to you in gratefulness for all you have done, are doing now, and will continue to do in our lives.

Conclusion

Gather the kindling. Strike the match. Allow the breeze of the Holy Spirit to ignite your faith.

Think about your faith. Where are you in this season of life? Is your faith alive, on fire, connected with God? Or do you struggle with hearing his voice and feeling his presence?

Living a life with a vibrant faith and a healthy spirituality requires ongoing formation of our faith God planted within each of us.

I hope at least one of the chapters in this book sparked your faith. Whenever you feel lost, dry, or in a rut, my prayer is you discover some idea in these pages to ignite your flame of faith once again.

Remember the quote at the beginning of the book:

I cannot cause light.
The most I can do is put myself in the path of its beam.
Annie Dillard

Move your soul into God's light and stir the embers of faith God gives each of us. Fuel your faith!

Blessing

As the Lord leads you from stuck to unstuck,
may you enjoy the comfort of his presence
and the warmth of his love.

Come near the heat of his spirit,
defrosting the chilliness of life.

Gather all the elements in your surroundings
kindling the blaze within your heart.

Savor the glow of his love and allow your being to
reflect his compassion onto others.

Enter God's light as he helps you
fan the flames of your faith.

Author Notes

I wrote this guidebook, not as a deep theological discussion about the elements of faith, but to be used as a quick reference when your faith is dim and your spirit sagging. The book is a reference to help you go back to the basics of prayer and study to energize your soul. Remember to try a new practice such as walking a labyrinth or writing in a journal. Find a practice to intensify your faith and bring you closer to God.

- Turn down page corners of ideas to try in the future.

- Write in the margins other ideas.

- Explore spiritual blogs, full of new approaches and fellow companions on this faith walk. I invite you to come to my blog: healthyspirituality.org

- You also may be interested in the books I write to help you along the way: Whispers, Being with God in Breath Prayers, Spiritual Retreats, a Guide to Slowing Down to be with God, 40 Voices, A Lenten Devotional and Christmas Crossroads, 30 Devotions for the Holiday Season.

- I am always adding more resources and ideas on the blog, healthyspirituality.org where I post weekly. Please subscribe so you don't miss out!

- Did you find this book helpful? Please take a minute to leave an honest review on Amazon. It is a wonderful way to say thank you to an author.

Interested in going deeper?

Let's connect and share our journeys together - companions and community spark faith too.

Beside my blog, you can find me:

My author's Facebook page, https://www.facebook.com/Jeanwiseauthor

Twitter https://twitter.com/Jeanwise

Pinterest https://www.pinterest.com/jeanwise22

Instagram: https://www.instagram.com/jeanwise/

About the Author

Jean Wise is a writer, speaker, retreat leader, and spiritual director. She is a contributor author of devotions for four compilations, as well as the author of several books. She has also written numerous devotionals, magazine articles, and newspaper features. You can find her books at healthyspirituality.org/amazon.

Jean is a Deacon at St. Peter's Lutheran Church facilitating adult spiritual formation. She has an active spiritual direction practice including leading group spiritual direction. She is a frequent speaker for gathering and retreats in northwest Ohio.

An RN with her Masters in Nursing, Jean retired from public health in 2006 as the County Health Commissioner to focus on freelance speaking and writing. She discovered her calling to nurture others, as she practiced in nursing, and now as she helps others grow closer to God in her ministry of spiritual direction, writing, and speaking.

She invites you to visit her blog where she writes two times a week: www.healthyspirituality.org and to connect on social media.

www.ingramcontent.com/pod-product-compliance
Lightning Source LLC
Chambersburg PA
CBHW071826020426
42331CB00007B/1618